SOUTHERN BIG TANKS:4

W 2-6-4Ts
31911-31925

Leslie Tibble

Irwell Press

Acknowledgements

Thanks in especial to Eric Youldon in the compilation of these notes; also to Brian Penney, Roger Merry-Price, Allan Baker, David Walker, Tony Wright, Brian Bailey and Mark Arscott. Richard Derry once again prepared the Tables; this time without the need to list shed allocations!

Printed by Newnorth Print, Bedford
Tel: 01525 861888
www.irwellpress.com

SOUTHERN BIG TANKS:4
W 2-6-4Ts
31911-31925

The last of the Southern 'Big Tanks' were three cylinder 2-6-4Ts; like the G16s, H16s and Zs, they were built for a very specific purpose. What was needed was a powerful loco with good acceleration. A tank engine would be preferable to a tender engine, for most journeys were short with frequent reversals; the traffic was goods between the London yards and all manner of cross London goods workings arising from them. The acceleration was required to get trains running through the commuter traffic and the power was necessary to overcome the many short local gradients; flyovers and suchlike and difficult starts from frequent signal stops. Maunsell arrived at a tank version of the N1 2-6-0, thus recreating the K1 2-6-4T of ill-starred River class association. No.890 RIVER FROME was the single three cylinder River tank and thus the progenitor of the N1 three-cylinder mogul. Ten such locos, the W class, were authorised in 1929 at a cost of some £9,000 each, to be built at

Eastleigh. As with the Zs, the timing was unfortunate; the Great Depression had dawned and, as the production of Zs had been curtailed, the Ws didn't get off the ground. Bradley records that five sets of frames and cylinders fabricated at Ashford were delivered to Eastleigh but they remained unused; five boilers from Brighton went similarly unused and were eventually used as spares for moguls. It was mid-1931 before a start was made on just five engines, 1911-1915 which emerged from Eastleigh in January-February 1932. This is C.S. Cocks in a paper to the Institution of Locomotive Engineers in 1949: *The W class tank engine, 2-6-4 type and virtually the K1 (Engine No.890) with 5ft 6in wheels, was built at Eastleigh Works and is based on the N1 three-cylinder locomotive with the addition of side tanks, bunker and trailing bogie. The cylinders are 16½in by 28in, the coupled wheels are 5ft 6in diameter and the boiler pressure is 200lb per sq inch, resulting in a tractive effort at 85% of the boiler pressure of 29,452lb and the adhesion factor*

in working order is 4.35 to 1 and 4 to 1 with half empty tanks and bunker. The leading truck is of the Cartazzi slide type. Some parts such as tanks, steps and elements of the bunkers, were re-used from the K and K1 tanks converted to 2-6-0s. Each tank held 620 gallons with the one in the bunker contributing 760 gallons giving a total of 2,000 gallons. A connection linked it to the side tanks, helping to support the cab. This wasn't visible as it was on the Urie H16 (*Big Tanks 2*). Water was taken through a filler alongside the firebox.

****

1911-1915 all went to Battersea Park, the old LBSC shed when new, for precisely the sort of work – principally cross-London freights – which had been envisaged back in 1929. There remained the batch of ten to finish the class as originally authorised but items for these locos were marooned as trade levels failed to improve and were instead used to make more moguls. In the

The first W, 1911 at its initial home, the old LBSCR sheds at Battersea Park on 4 February 1933. Steam escaping from sniffing valves on smokebox. One of the earliest reports concerned 1912 'at Battersea Park shed, 'working freight out of Battersea Yard to Norwood via Crystal Palace, returning to Battersea via Thornton Heath.' In addition, it and other Ws at Battersea were working via the West London Line between Old Oak and Norwood Junction, on heavy coal trains. The three lamp headcode covered a group of cross-London routes. By 1936 the class was distributed as follows: 1911-1914 at Stewarts Lane then routinely called – confusingly – Battersea; 1915-1920 at Norwood Junction; 1921-1925 at Hither Green. H.C. Casserley, courtesy R.M. Casserley.

General Arrangement Drawing Maunsell W 2-6-4T

In the official title '(R.H.D.)' means Right-Hand Drive, so the drawing strictly applies to 31911-31915.

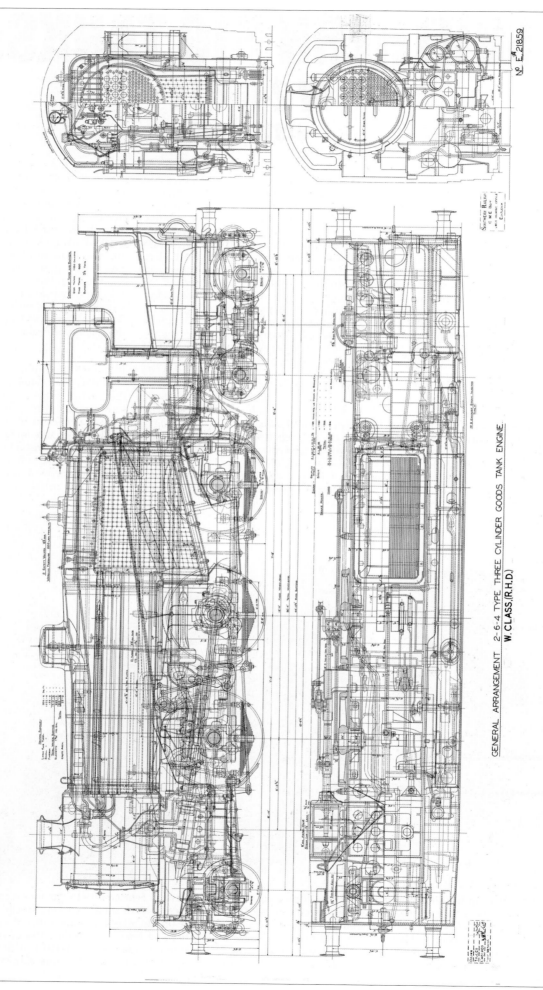

GENERAL ARRANGEMENT 2-6-4 TYPE THREE CYLINDER GOODS TANK ENGINE.
W. CLASS. (R.H.D.)

1919 at Norwood Junction shed 10 April 1937. The exposed reversing arm, inside the tank cutaway, was later partly covered. H.C. Casserley, courtesy R.M. Casserley.

BRITISH RAILWAYS and BR numbers in Gill sans early on, newly applied to 31919, seen at Norwood Junction on 5 December 1948. R.C. Riley, transporttreasury

The arrangement of shunters step and hand rail, as well as the steam braking to the bogie wheels, at the rear of 31915 at Stewarts Lane; 1911-1915 were built at Eastleigh with right-hand drive while 1916-1925 were built at Ashford, with left-hand drive. The right-hand locos had the vacuum brake ejector exhaust pipe, running from the cab front to the smokebox on the right-hand side. The shunters step and hand rail were on the left-hand, namely the fireman's, side. The left-hand locos had the vacuum brake ejector exhaust pipe, running from the cab front to the smokebox on the left-hand side. The shunters step and hand rail were then on the right-hand, namely the fireman's, side. The electrification flash is off-set to match the grab iron that side.

meantime, in 1930 five more had been authorised so that by 1935 – six years on in the W story as it were – ten more were still awaited. As it was they all came out that year and the following year, from Ashford works. Most of them went to Hither Green for just the sort of yard to yard freight that the first five had been working since 1932. To a remarkable degree the fifteen Ws remained in the geographical confines of the London built up area; in this way they were 'parochial' like the G16s and H16s and for years it was only the Zs among the engines in this volume that 'travelled'. Until 1962 that is…

The first, Eastleigh batch of five had gravity sanding and right-hand drive, while the later Ashford batch of ten had steam sanding and left-hand drive. The first batch was fitted with steam sanding in 1959-60 but kept the right-hand drive.

In 1948 despite years of reluctance to employ the type, 2-6-4Ts began trials on the Southern Region with a pair transferred from the LMR. This led to their widespread use until eventually replaced by the BR Standard version. The story goes that someone 'higher up' wanted to know what was wrong with the Southern's own home-grown 2-6-4Ts; the Fairburn 2-6-4Ts were undergoing SR trials in April 1948 and the following month W 1918 mysteriously and unprecedentedly

turned up at Victoria with a special from Tunbridge Wells West. 2-6-4Ts were certainly flavour of the month, for it was even rumoured that ER L1s would be put on trial – their arrival was even confidently predicted, on 26 June 1948. They never did turn up and the decision was made in the meantime to build Fairburn tanks at Brighton. The W, now 31918, did do another trial, however, working a six coach train from Ashford to Tonbridge on 11 May 1948. It fair rattled off the 26-odd miles at nearly 60mph but ran alarmingly hot; this, apparently, despite Ashford Works specially preparing it. Nothing further was heard of Ws on passenger work, but see 31915 later.

At November 1945 the allocation was as follows:
1911 Hither Green
1912 Stewarts Lane
1913 Hither Green
1914 Stewarts Lane
1915 Stewarts Lane
1916 Norwood Junction
1917 Norwood Junction
1918 Norwood Junction
1919 Norwood Junction
1920 Norwood Junction
1921 Hither Green
1922 Hither Green
1923 Hither Green
1924 Hither Green
1925 Hither Green

Ten years later, in June 1955 it had barely changed.
31911 Hither Green
31912 Hither Green
31913 Hither Green
31914 Stewarts Lane
31915 Stewarts Lane
31916 Hither Green
31917 Norwood Junction
31918 Norwood Junction
31919 Norwood Junction
31920 Norwood Junction
31921 Stewarts Lane
31922 Hither Green
31923 Hither Green
31924 Hither Green
31925 Hither Green

At the end of the *Big Tanks 3* the doom of the Zs was heralded by the sighting of a solitary locomotive on the afternoon of 23 September 1962; a W 2-6-4T, 31924 hitherto unknown in The West passing light westwards through Crewkerne, 'destination unknown'. As said at the close of the previous section, wholesale replacement had been planned and was duly enacted; all the Zs were withdrawn by the end of 1962, replaced by the somewhat less suitable (it was generally agreed) W 2-6-4Ts. 31924 reached Exmouth Junction shed the next day. It was undergoing clearance tests at St David's and Central on 8 October but was then stabled cold at Exmouth Junction shed. By the end of the month however, it was on the

The right-hand big end of 31915. The W tanks clearly had 'reversed' coupling rods, with the knuckle joint *ahead* of the crank pin of the reversed rods and therefore more awkward to get at. Note the unusual design of the leading footstep. R.A. Yeomans, transporttreasury

31911 on one of the endless cross-London freights which so occupied the class; bunker-first at Kensington, 18 August 1956. Because of the Sevenoaks derailment of the River Class 2-6-4T, the Ws were in effect banned from passenger workings, the only time they'd haul carriages being empty-stock diagrams. R.C. Riley, transporttreasury

banking work, together with 31921, though two or three Zs were still active. More Ws arrived before the year was out.

At the end of January 1963 the W listing was very different:

31911 Exmouth Junction
31912 Exmouth Junction
31913 Norwood Junction**
31914 Exmouth Junction
31915 Exmouth Junction
31916 Exmouth Junction
31917 Feltham**
31918 Norwood Junction
31919 Norwood Junction
31920 Norwood Junction
31921 Norwood Junction
31922 Feltham
31923 *
31924 Exmouth Junction
31925 Norwood Junction

*Was transferred to Exmouth Junction in January 1963 but condemned before it arrived.
**Had come to Exmouth Junction but were found surplus and sent back to the SR.

Richard Derry writes: *Tank engines based on the N1 three cylinder moguls, the Ws in my spotting days remained something of a mystery and even travelling around London to the main running sheds and the larger stations for a long time never came across them; two years in which their little section in the Ian Allan abcs remained stubbornly blank. They kept to well trodden paths, which sadly didn't include our 'home turf' at Weybridge or anywhere near it; worse the places where they would be found were reportedly unsympathetic in the extreme to number-taking oiks. Oddly, we found the North London MPDs more accommodating; it wasn't until it was too late that I visited Hither Green and Stewarts Lane and I never tried to get past the foremen at Bricklayers Arms or Norwood Junction. So it was that the Ws seemed as remote to me as the Beattie well tanks then at Wadebridge in deepest Cornwall and I visualised the whole of the class being withdrawn before I could see any of them due to the advancement of the Kent Coast electrification.*

Walton-on-Thames boys school had the usual trainspotters' grapevine though it was not entirely trustworthy; one or two miscreants would tell porkies and I fell for a couple of these. In the spring of 1961 the rumour went round that a class W had been seen on Feltham shed at weekends and not just off a goods from the Eastern section.

My attempted visits there however had always been abruptly terminated with the shout of 'Oi!' followed by 'Go away' or something similar. There was another attempt on the mystical W the next Sunday, ending in the same result, a few numbers written down, no W and a hasty retreat. In other words the usual outcome, a long bike ride and once again, no new numbers. Even some of the lads from the Weybridge 'Haines Bridge' mob who went to other schools had picked up on this rumour so at the evening attendance we speculated whether the two 70B goods duties that passed under the bridge would turn up a class W; no, it was always one of the local S15 4-6-0s.

The whole subject came to a head one mid-week lunchtime at school; flying visits to Hersham station were possible but only if you were on first sitting for lunch. Well this day I decided not to go; rarely did anything new turn up and the 'Bournemouth Belle' always had a well-thumbed local Bulleid Pacific at the head. On the arrival back of a group from the station (always before 1.25pm, otherwise – detention) I scoffed that they were out with the porkies again. A class W had run light engine on the down slow, 31911 on its way to a new home at Eastleigh MPD. Actually

31913 at Hither Green shed on 28 March 1959, still with first emblem. The below-running plate detail is interesting in the absence of the connecting rod, taken inside for attention. The missing connecting road makes clear the position of the knuckle joint ahead of the crank pin of the 'reversed' coupling rods – remarked upon on the previous page. That pipe emerging from the right-hand side of the smokebox was not present at first; moreover it could vary in length... There was more to come with grab irons and piping at the front of the W tanks; see throughout and 31922 on 5 September 1959 for instance. R.C. Riley, transporttreasury

SOME DUTIES
Hither Green/Winter 1957.
Duties covered were 203, 204, 206, 207, 208 and 209
Samples 203 and 209

Duty No.203
Departed HG loco light engine at 9.20am
Departed Hither Green [A.Section] on goods at 9.50am
Arrived Willesden at 11.40am, departed unspecified time, light engine
Arrived Sudbury Sidings at unspecified time, departed on goods at 1.50pm
Arrived Hither Green sidings at 3.37pm, then light engine Hither Green loco
Departed Hither Green loco light engine at 11.55pm
Arrived Hither Green [A.Section], departed on goods at 12.15am
Arrived Willesden at 2.10am, departed unspecified time, light engine
Arrived Sudbury Sidings at unspecified time, departed on goods at 4am
Arrived Hither Green sidings at 5.52am, then light engine to Hither Green loco.
Inter-regional transfer goods worked by Hither Green men.

Duty No.209
Departed HG loco light engine at 12.40am
Departed Hither Green [C.Section] on goods at 1.05am
Arrived Sevenoaks at 2.25am, departed on goods at 3.45am
Arrived Hither Green sidings at 5.15am, departed on goods at 6.15am
Arrived Down yard at 6.30am, then light engine to HG loco
Departed HG loco light engine at 11.08am
Departed Hither Green [A.Section] on goods at 11.28am
Arrived Feltham at 1.14pm' departed on goods at 2.22pm
Arrived Hither Green at 4.10pm, then light engine to HG loco.
Hither Green men did a night trip to Sevenoaks, returned and then a transfer trip to Feltham Yard.
An early and night set of men were used.

Norwood Junction/Winter 1960.
Duties 584, 586 and 587 were worked
Sample 586

Duty No.586
Departed Norwood loco, light engine at 5.10am
Departed Norwood yard, on goods at 5.30am
Arrived at Epsom goods at 7.34am, goods shunting from 8.30am to 11.15am
Departed Epsom goods on goods train at 11.32am
Arrived Norwood up yard at 12.06pm, then light engine to Norwood loco
Departed Norwood loco, light engine at 10.30pm
Arrived at East Croydon [via Selhurst] at 10.37pm, departed on goods at 11.08pm
Arrived Battersea yard [via Crystal Palace] at 11.48pm, departed on goods at 12.45am
Arrived Norwood yard at 1.31am, then light engine to Norwood loco.
Norwood men worked local goods and shunted with a long layover in the afternoon on Norwood loco. Two sets of men were used.

Stewarts Lane/Winter 1960.
Duty no.514 OFF no.513
Departed Norwood shed [having arrive at 5.55am] light engine at 9.35am
departed Norwood down yard on goods at 9.50am
Arrived Wallington 10.14am, departed light engine 10.53am
Arrived Norwood up yard [via Selhurst] 11.06am departed on goods at 11.43am
Arrived Battersea yard [via Crystal Palace] 12.18pm, departed on goods at 1.30pm
Arrived Norwood down yard 2.09pm departed on goods at 2.35pm
Arrived Waddon Marsh 2.57pm, departed light engine 3.30pm
Arrived Norwood loco 3.50pm, departed light engine 12.05am
Arrived Norwood up yard 12.15am, departed on goods at 12.30am, via Selhurst, West London Line and Gospel Oak
Arrived Ferme Park at 2.30am, departed on goods at 4am
Arrived Battersea yard at 5.55am, departed light engine at 6.10am and arrived at Stewarts Lane loco at 6.20am.
Then worked duty No.513 [details available if required].
Two sets of Norwood men had all the work which included local goods and an inter-regional transfer night working to Ferme Park, Eastern Region. The train ran via Selhurst, the West London line, Willesden Jct. Gospel Oak and the T and H line to Ferme Park via Harringay West Jct.

How banking works. 31914 and 31915 pushing a stone train out of St David's on 2 July 1963. R.C. Riley, transporttreasury

Bread and butter work, coal trains through the London suburbs, never seen by the rush hour crowds. This is Crystal Palace Low Level, platforms 7/8, 31914 running through with a late morning coal working, 12 March 1954. R.C. Riley, transporttreasury

it was p/e 26/5/61, and it had been a Hither Green loco for over twelve years. To say I was downcast hardly conveys the impact of this particular childhood trauma. I desperately hoped it was a hoax/group hysteria, recalling my own shame, convinced I'd seen D846 STEADFAST some time before it actually entered service – on a school trip to the RHDR of all things. Appallingly, they were correct, so more regular visits to Hersham station ensued which at least now offered the possibility of one of the new E5000 electrics then just entering service. But I eventually got my reward, 31913, another transfer to Eastleigh shed at a time when a number of the class were moving over to the Western section to Eastleigh and Feltham.

For a few years from the birth of BR the W 2-6-4Ts remained at their traditional homes, Hither Green, Stewarts Lane and Norwood Junction. History shows us how they moved on in the face of Modernisation before eventually surrendering to the scrapman. I never did see all of them but only missed 31915 on its way to Exmouth Junction shed towards the end 1962 and 31919 and 31921 both late of Norwood Junction.

31913 (1913)

Built Eastleigh Works. To traffic 30/1/32
Renumbered 3/9/49

Boilers
No.1060 from new
No.878 3/6/37
No.899 19/8/44
No.1063 3/9/49
No.1062 14/2/55
No.1014 26/9/59

Shed allocations
New to Stewarts Lane
Hither Green 1/4/48
Eastleigh 26/5/61
Exmouth Jct 19/11/62
Norwood Jct 25/1/63
Feltham 6/1/64

Works

27/3/33-19/5/53**C**	At Brighton Works
3/5/34-29/5/34**C**	At Stewarts Lane shed
23/5/35-4/6/35**C**	52,854 At Stewarts Lane shed
6/9/35-11/11/35**C**	56,218
13/4/37-3/6/37**A**	74,281
26/9/39-4/10/39**C**	39,426 Class plate fitted, extension of mileage 5,000
10/10/39**C**	39,448 At Stewarts Lane shed
2/7/41-6/8/41**C**	67,025
22/4/42-6/6/42**C**	78,157 Extension of mileage 10,000
4/7/44-19/8/44**A**	118,244 337 copper and 228 roof stays renewed, lead plugs renewed, new large steel tubes with copper ends
14/6/46-10/7/46**C**	No mileage recorded, all small tubes renewed at Hither Green shed
15/7/47-9/8/47**C**	49,347
22/7/49-3/9/49**A**	77,727 Renumbered, 228 roof stays renewed, internal tubes renewed
17/7/50-1/8/50**LI**	15,169 No boiler work. First BR emblem
14/5/52-30/5/52**LI**	42,337 270 nuts renewed, 173 new tubes 'Howells', 3 large tubes repaired with copper ends
20/1/55-14/2/55**GO**	87,965 500 copper stays riveted over, 210 nuts renewed, 16 studs filled in laps, 173 new tubes 'Universal'.
16/11/56-7/12/56**HI**	31,798
18/2/57-27/2/57**LC**	33,222
26/8/59-26/9/59**GO**	71,512 Fitted with steam sanding, handrails in front of engine, cast iron firebars. Second BR emblem
1/10/60-9/11/60 **LC**	At Bricklayers Arms shops
29/1/63-9/2/63**LC**	37,567 2 fusible plugs, 173 new tubes 'Tube Products' 21 new large tubes, at Eastleigh Works

Withdrawn 1/3/64, cut up at Birds, Morriston, Swansea

All work at Ashford Works unless otherwise stated	**LI Light Intermediate**
No detail for first few years.	
Extent of overhauls not specified until BR days but	**HI Heavy Intermediate**
General overhauls, say, can be inferred from boiler	**G General**
changes.	**LC Light Casual**
Inverted commas = trade name of component	**NC Non-Classified**
Ret = Return for rectification	
SR designations: A - General, B - Intermediate, C - Casual, D - Non-classified.	

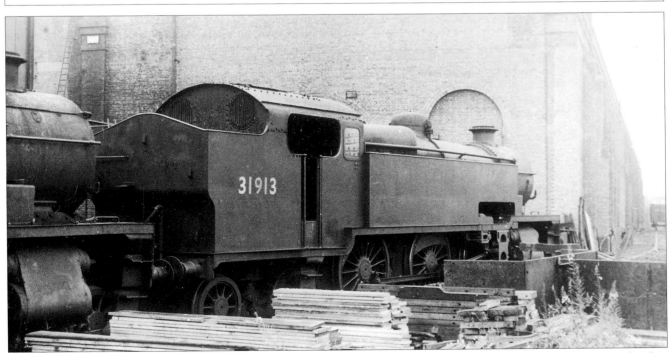

In for a Light Intermediate at Ashford Works, 15 July 1950; snifting valves gone in meantime. It would soon get the first emblem. H.C. Casserley, courtesy R.M. Casserley.

31913 at Hither Green shed, 23 July 1955. The buffer beam arrangement is strikingly similar to that of the Z 0-8-0Ts, the beam proper (with the drawhook) resting squarely and conventionally on the end of the frames, the upper part being simply a plate. The square bolted plate is obviously for access – presumably to remove the valve of the inside cylinder. transporttreasury

Stored at Feltham shed, 7 April 1964, after withdrawal a few weeks before. Peter Groom.

31913 on the coaling road at Norwood Junction, March 1963. BR second emblem, electrification flashes. J. Kirke, transporttreasury

27

31914 (a Stewarts Lane engine at the time) sits in the siding that so often held an engine off the transfer jobs there, on 10 May 1959. A glimpse for once of the arrangement of lifting lugs, fire iron retaining pieces and the solid line of rivets where the tank is alongside the boiler. Look as you might, the water filler cap is *never* visible; it is on top of the tank below the dome. R.C. Riley, transporttreasury

31917 (1917)

Built at Ashford Works. To traffic 3/5/35
Renumbered 11/11/49

Boilers
No.1087 from new
No.1039 7/5/41
No.1060 28/6/47
No.1083 1/8/53
No.1080 18/4/58

Shed allocations
New to Stewarts Lane
Norwood Jct 8/1935
Exmouth Jct 19/11/62
Feltham 25/1/63

Works

4/6/35-17/6/35**D**	503	
9/10/35-5/12/35**C**	3,648	
11/8/37-21/9/37**C**	30,281 173 nuts renewed, All small and all large tubes renewed	
23/6/39-28/7/39**B**	53,058 Class plate fitted, extension of mileage 20,000, new middle and left hand cylinder, all small tubes renewed, 'Tubes ltd'	
11/4/41-7/5/41**A**	79,431	
11/11/43-7/12/43**C**	37,700	
9/10/44-15/11/44**C**	At Norwood Jct shed	
22/3/46-14/5/46**C**	At Norwood Jct shed	
30/5/47-28/6/47**A**	91,622	
18/10/49-11/11/49**LI**	38,002 Renumbered, 7 copper stays renewed, 6 small tubes repaired	
1/5/51-25/5/51**HI**	59,406 4 copper stays repaired, 550 copper stays riveted over, 24 nuts renewed, 23 copper studs fitted in laps, 173 new small tubes, 'Howells'. First BR emblem	
31/5/51-13/6/51**Defect**		
20/11/51-13/12/51**Ret**	80 copper stays renewed	
9/7/53-1/8/53**GO**	88,996 825 copper stays repaired, 705 steel stays and 705 nuts renewed, New firebox	
17/9/53**Ret**	537	
13/3/56-6/4/56**LI**	46,977 38 copper stays riveted over, 208 nuts renewed, 2 fusible plugs	
19/3/58-18/4/58**GO**	80,007 150 copper stays renewed, 576 monel metal stays renewed, 576 nuts renewed, 38 roof nuts renewed, 2 fusible plugs. Second BR emblem	
24/6/60-14/7/60**LC**	37,090	
11/3/63-15/3/63**NC**	At Bricklayers Arms shops	

Withdrawn 5/1/64, cut up at Birds, Morriston, Swansea

All work at Ashford Works unless otherwise stated	LI Light Intermediate
No detail for first few years.	
Extent of overhauls not specified until BR days but	HI Heavy Intermediate
General overhauls, say, can be inferred from boiler	G General
changes.	LC Light Casual
Inverted commas = trade name of component	NC Non-Classified
Ret=Return for rectification	
SR designations: A - General, B - Intermediate, C - Casual, D - Non-classified.	

31917 with an animated crew at Feltham shed, 23 June 1963; one of the earlier 'Big Tanks' is over on the right. 31917 is one of the ten with left-hand drive, so the shunters step and rail are on the right. ColourRail

31918 at Norwood Junction shed on 10 November 1957; a wisp of steam escapes from the bogie steam brake. R.C. Riley, transporttreasury

31918 working what looks like a train of scrap, a down freight passing North Pole Junction signal box, 8 August 1959. R.C. Riley, transporttreasury

31923 alongside the Repair Hall at Feltham MPD, 13 March 1961, a period when all the H16s were away at Eastleigh. 31923 was the only W not to get the second BR emblem. Note the repeated patching on the tank – some patches overlap earlier ones so it was a persistent problem! Peter Groom.

1924 at Ashford shed, 10 April 1937. H.C. Casserley, courtesy R.M. Casserley.

31925 (1925)

Built at Ashford Works. To traffic 3/4/36
Renumbered 10/6/48

Boilers
No.1069 from new
No.1067 6/6/42
No.1044 10/6/48
No.1160 17/4/53
No.999 6/6/59

Shed allocations
Hither Green from new
Norwood Jct 26/5/61

Works

27/10/36-20/11/36**C**	7,356 At Brighton Works, 17 copper stays riveted over	
20/10/38-16/11/38**C**	38,693 At Brighton Works	
2/10/39-31/10/39**C**	51,993 At Bricklayers Arms shops, all small tubes renewed	
13/7/40-10/8/40**C**	63,842 At Bricklayers Arms shops	
15/4/42-6/6/42**A**	84,899 89 copper renewed and 150 copper stays riveted over, 438 nuts renewed, 2 flange patches fitted, 4 small tube holes plugged	
20/2/45-9/3/45**C**	At Hither Green shed, 169 new small tubes, 'New Steel'	
25/9/45-15/9/45**B**	56,548	
25/9/46-9/11/46**D**	72,124	
22/4/48-10/6/48**A**	Renumbered, 94 copper renewed and 100 copper stays riveted over, 311 nuts renewed, 52 rivets caulked, 21 large tubes repaired	
7/3/51-6/4/51**LI**	44,922 50 copper stays riveted over, 5 nuts renewed, 2 fusible plugs, all new small tubes. First BR emblem	
15/4/52-2/5/52**LC**	60,874	
23/3/53-17/4/53**GO**	76,372	
8/5/53**Ret**		
10/8/53-25/8/53**NC**	3,561	
5/5/54-22/5/54**HC**	13,509, 173 new small tubes, 'Howells'	
27/5/54-28/5/54		
6/7/55-14/7/55**LC**	30,866	
12/12/56-5/1/57**HI**	54,803, 5 copper renewed and 63 copper stays riveted over, 45 nuts renewed, 2 fusible plugs, 173 new small tubes 'Stewart and Lloyds', electrically welded	
5/5/59-6/6/59**GO**	91,400. Second BR emblem	
2/1/61-28/2/61**LC**	At Bricklayers Arms shops	
6/12/61-22/12/61**LC**	28,426	

Withdrawn 9/11/63. Cut up at Eastleigh Works 25/1/64

All work at Ashford Works unless otherwise stated	LI Light Intermediate
No detail for first few years.	
Extent of overhauls not specified until BR days but	HI Heavy Intermediate
General overhauls, say, can be inferred from boiler	G General
changes.	LC Light Casual
Inverted commas = trade name of component	NC Non-Classified
Ret=Return for rectification	
SR designations: A - General, B - Intermediate, C - Casual, D - Non-classified.	

31925 at Hither Green in the mid-1950s. ColourRail

With right-hand drive companion at Hither Green, 19 October 1957. B.K.B. Green, Initial Photographics.

31925 with second emblem, at Hither Green on 21 February 1960. The reversing shaft and the bracket holding it in place this side is clear to see for once, in that opening in the tank. R.C. Riley, transporttreasury

31925 with a freight, not in the Garden of England, but in its usual London haunts – almost certainly on the down slow line at Wandsworth Common, just before the curve into the station, about 1962.

At Hither Green on 27 April 1958, with a glimpse of the reversing shaft again through that gap in the tank. Peter Groom.

The most substantial footsteps ever devised – in the true tradition of Urie! R.A. Yeomans, transporttreasury